Pebble™ Plus

Under the Sea

# Octopuses

by Carol K. Lindeen

Consulting Editor: Gail Saunders-Smith, PhD

Consultant: Jody Rake, Member
Southwest Marine/Aquatic Educators' Association

Capstone press

Mankato, Minnesota

Pebble Plus is published by Capstone Press,
151 Good Counsel Drive, P.O. Box 669, Mankato, Minnesota 56002.
www.capstonepress.com

*Library of Congress Cataloging-in-Publication Data*
Lindeen, Carol K., 1976–
    Octopuses / by Carol K. Lindeen.
    p. cm.—(Pebble Plus—Under the Sea)
    Includes bibliographical references and index.
    ISBN 0-7368-3661-6 (hardcover)
    1. Octopuses—Juvenile literature. I. Title. II. Series.
QL430.3.O2L56 2005
594'.56—dc22                                            2004011098

Summary: Simple text and photographs present octopuses, their body parts, and their behavior.

**Editorial Credits**
Martha E. H. Rustad, editor; Juliette Peters, set designer; Kate Opseth, book designer; Kelly Garvin,
    photo researcher; Scott Thoms, photo editor

**Photo Credits**
Corbis/Royalty-Free, cover
Jeff Rotman, 10–11, 18–19
Michael Patrick O'Neill, 12–13
Minden Pictures/Chris Newbert, 4–5
Seapics.com/David B. Fleetham, 9; John C. Lewis, 1, 16–17; Marc Chamberlain, 14–15;
    Reinhard Dirscheri, 6–7, 20–21

## Note to Parents and Teachers

The Under the Sea set supports national science standards related to the diversity
and unity of life. This book describes and illustrates octopuses. The images support
early readers in understanding the text. The repetition of words and phrases helps early
readers learn new words. This book also introduces early readers to subject-specific
vocabulary words, which are defined in the Glossary section. Early readers may need
assistance to read some words and to use the Table of Contents, Glossary, Read More,
Internet Sites, and Index sections of the book.

# Table of Contents

# What Are Octopuses?

Octopuses are animals that swim near the ocean floor.

Most octopuses are smaller
than people.

# Body Parts

Octopuses have eight tentacles.

The tentacles are joined

to their heads.

Octopuses have suckers

on their tentacles.

Suckers hold on to food.

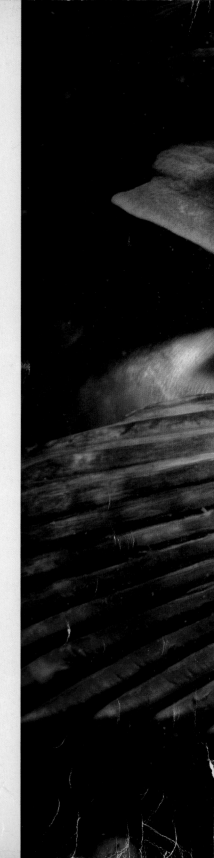

Octopuses have two big eyes.

They can see well

in the water.

# What Octopuses Do

Octopuses live in dens.

They hide from other animals

in their dens.

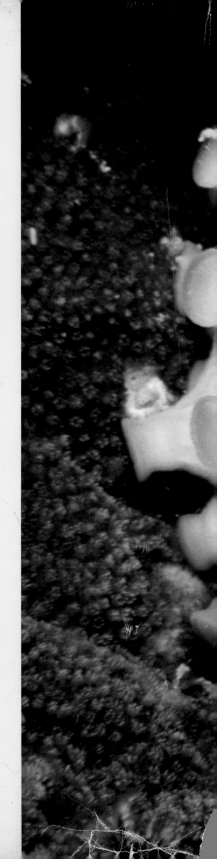

Octopuses change their colors
to hide from other animals.

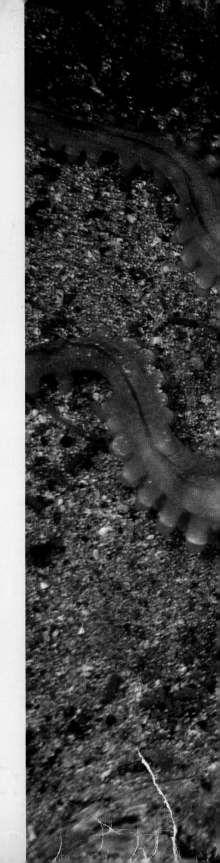

Octopuses squirt ink.
The ink hides them
from other animals.

# Under the Sea

Octopuses squirt water out
of their bodies to move.
Octopuses swim
under the sea.

# Glossary

den—an animal's home; octopuses make dens in coral reefs or under rocks.

ink—a dark liquid; an octopus shoots ink into the water to hide itself from other animals.

squirt—to shoot a liquid out quickly

sucker—a soft, flexible part on an animal's body that is used to cling on to something

tentacle—a long, flexible arm of an animal; octopuses use their tentacles to move, feel, and hold.

# Read More

**Roop, Connie, and Peter Roop.** *Octopus under the Sea.* Hello Science Reader! New York: Scholastic, 2001.

**Swanson, Diane.** *Octopuses.* Welcome to the World of Animals. Milwaukee: Gareth Stevens, 2002.

**Zuchora-Walske, Christine.** *Giant Octopuses.* Pull Ahead Books Minneapolis: Lerner, 2000.

# Internet Sites

FactHound offers a safe, fun way to find Internet sites related to this book. All of the sites on FactHound have been researched by our staff.

Here's how:

1. Visit *www.facthound.com*

2. Type in this special code **0736836616** for age-appropriate sites. Or enter a search word related to this book for a more general search.

3. Click on the **Fetch It** button.

FactHound will fetch the best sites for you!

# Index

Word Count: 94
Grade Level: 1
Early-Intervention Level: 11